Bruce and
Nancy Roberts

WHERE TIME STOOD STILL

CROWELL-COLLIER PRESS
DIVISION OF MACMILLAN PUBLISHING CO., INC.
NEW YORK
COLLIER MACMILLAN PUBLISHERS
LONDON

2 - 26 - 74

Photographs from Rapho Guillumette Pictures.
First photograph courtesy of *Friends Magazine*.

This book is dedicated
to the people of Appalachia
and to those who help them

CONTENTS

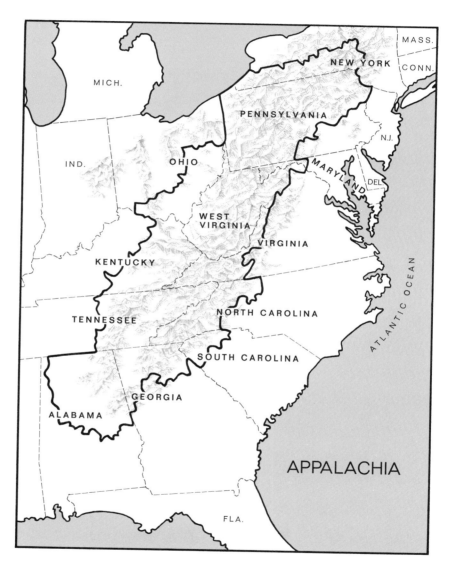

*The Southern Appalachian Region includes some 80,000 square miles in
North Carolina, South Carolina, Tennessee, Kentucky, Georgia, Virginia,
West Virginia, and Alabama. The United States Government Appalachian
Regional Commission Report of 1965 also includes certain counties of
Ohio, Pennsylvania, New York, and Maryland to enable those states to
take advantage of federal aid grants, but it is the southern region, the
subject of this book, that is most commonly designated* Appalachia

WHERE TIME STOOD STILL

1. ADVENTURERS IN THE WILDERNESS

The story is still told in the Appalachian Mountains of the young man who abducted his sweetheart because her family opposed their marriage. He carried her away with him deep into the mountains and built a cabin for his bride at the edge of a dense forest. One day several years later, when her husband was out hunting, she decided to go berry picking. She wandered farther and farther into the woods in search of berries and finally, as she crossed a stream, saw a cabin a short distance away. To her surprise she recognized the home of her parents! For five years she had been living only three miles from her family, unknown to them or to her.

Even today distances seem longer than they actually are on the winding mountain roads of Appalachia. For many years the lack of roads and the natural difficulties of travel through mountain areas resulted in isolation for those who lived there. Thus generation after generation of children grew up, married, and raised their own families, never leaving the immediate area of their birth.

Listening to the voices of the mountain people, one still hears traces of an Elizabethan accent like faint echoes from their pioneer past.

Today, the term Appalachia often suggests only poverty, but it means much more, for this was the first frontier of our country. A wilderness filled with beauty, it was also a place of danger and hardships. If the settlers survived Indian raids, there was still the threat of smallpox and malaria. The challenge to survive was great, and those who accepted it were a new breed, unafraid and ready to risk all.

Many of them came from England, Scotland, Ireland, Germany, or France. The majority were Protestants, strongly imbued with the individualistic traits of their faith and a desire for religious freedom. Not always literate, they might best be described as a courageous, sometimes ornery people determined to live life in their own way. Somehow they did, and somehow they managed to survive.

The first settlers literally lived off the land, eating Indian corn, berries, and wild game. Their possessions were often limited to an ax, a knife, a rifle, and a loom. But even during those early days, these men and women never considered themselves poor. For they owned land, and this had not always been possible in Europe.

It was their land that gave them a feeling of worth, a sense of pride and of being men among men. A basic need was fulfilled, and to this day natives of Appalachia do not consider themselves poor so long as they can call a few acres of land their own.

Having pushed into the mountains by the time of the American Revolution, they raised large families in the shelter of the coves and valleys, often naming their settlements after the families who lived there. Game was abundant, the valleys fertile, the climate mild, and the country was beautiful.

The land seemed to cast a spell over its people. Spring was and still is an unforgettable succession of wildflowers, from the first feathery white blooms of the "sarvis" to the purple mist of the redbud trees to the later profusion of white dogwood. Throughout the forests may be found every shade of green in the spectrum. Along with the new leaves come the startling beauty of the wild flame azalea, vast stretches of laurel thick with tiny pink blossoms, and spectacular pink and red rhododendrons covering entire mountainsides with a mass of color.

If these people who loved their mountains so well could not leave them in the spring, how could they do so in the fall when they resemble the palette of an absent-minded painter who has allowed one brilliant color to flow into another. Summer rains and mists are gone, and over this dazzling display is an intensely blue autumn sky ablaze at dusk with the most dramatic sunsets of the year.

It is now over three hundred years since pioneers first settled the recesses of the Appalachian Mountains, and thousands of the descendants of these frontiersmen are still there. Hospitable

and essentially honest, they care little for physical comforts and they enjoy their solitude.

In time of war, the mountain men responded to the call to fight and served their country well, but afterward most returned to the hills whence they had come. Some were unable to make a place for themselves in the unfamiliar, highly competitive outside world while others preferred to go back to a way of life that allowed them to live close to the land with plenty of space around them.

This is not a land that has attracted black immigrants. Most of Appalachia's population is native-born and descended from early white settlers. The mountain people are clannish, and it takes considerable time before either the white or black stranger feels at home or accepted.

2. PEOPLE OF APPALACHIA

Among the early settlers of western North Carolina was a man named Samuel Hicks. He had many descendants, and the Hicks name is well known today in the Wautauga and Avery county area. One of these descendants is Albert Hicks who lives with his family near the North Carolina-Tennessee border.

Lucy Mae and Albert Hicks are fortunate enough to live on a paved road, but there are no close neighbors with whom they can socialize and the children have no playmates nearby. Since the children have only a few "play-pretties," they invent many games. These may consist of placing on end some tiles they have found until one tile topples, causing the others to fall in a uniform row; using a log that their father has placed over a piece of wood as a seesaw; jumping rope; climbing trees; or exploring Cranberry Creek, which winds along behind their small frame house. The creek makes little silvery waterfalls over the rocks and by midsummer, when its icy waters have warmed, the children will wade in search of tadpoles, or fish hopefully for trout.

Sheila, sixteen, Brenda, fourteen, Frieda, eleven, and Billy, eight, all live at home with their parents. The oldest Hicks boy, twenty-year-old Bobby Joe, is away at a diesel school in Tennessee. There are few local opportunities for specialized training.

When Albert Hicks was a freckle-faced, tow-headed boy of seven, his mother died. While his father worked, Albert fed the family's two pigs and milked the cow. But after his mother's death there was no longer anyone at home to help tend the vegetable garden or can the colorful jars of tomatoes, corn, beans, and kraut, which provide necessary food for mountain families during the long winters.

The fifth grade was Albert's last year of school. "Times were hard for dad and me, so I started working at a sawmill," says Mr. Hicks. Although he was not yet twelve years old, Albert worked ten hours a day at the mill. These were the years of the Depression. But with the exception of coal-mining towns, the Depression was not such a shock to Appalachia. Since its people had never known wealth or easy money, there was no sudden drop in their standard of living. "Life was tough, yes, but it

Albert Hicks

The Hicks family: Billy, Sheila, Mrs. Hicks, Brenda (standing), and Frieda

always was a struggle to get food, buy clothes, and just stay alive." The coming of the Depression only made the struggle a little more desperate. "Dad got on with the WPA and I don't know what we'd have done without that. It saved us."

The WPA (Works Project Administration) was the Federal agency which, during the Depression, employed most of the idle mountaineers to construct schools, roads, improve water supplies, and even build sanitary privies in an effort to raise health standards. Now, thirty years later, incomes are still low compared to the rest of the nation, with the average Appalachian family making between $2,000 and $3,000 a year. "And what with prices going up all the time a dollar doesn't go far these days," says Mr. Hicks.

To make matters worse, Albert Hicks suffered the blow a man trying to support a wife and five children dreads most — poor health. Surgeons had to remove a large part of his stomach and recovery was slow. He was often unable to work.

"Now, I'm getting back on my feet and we're doing all right." He has gotten a job that he likes driving a rock picker at a nearby resort where a golf course is being carved out of the base of the mountains. Last year he made $2,400 and hopes to do better this year.

For those not lucky enough to have a steady job, there is a short time in the fall when money is to be made picking apples. Small farmers sometimes add to their income by going out with their families to gather mountain laurel, which is shipped to florists. The steep hillsides do not lend themselves to profitable large-scale farming, and the thin, rocky top soil in many areas is more receptive to the hand hoe than the mechanical cultivator.

Uncle Jim Beard, Albert Hicks's uncle, spent most of his life farming a few acres of land and sometimes digging a little "sang" (ginseng). For years drug companies have bought this root, which is shaped like the human body, and shipped it to Hong Kong. The Chinese have believed in its medicinal value for centuries and are convinced it has a tranquilizing effect. Many a mountain herb digger has his own secret places back in the

Uncle Jim Beard (center)
and the woman the Beards
took in as a child (right)

shady forests where he goes to gather this little plant with its three large and two small leaves. More than two hundred crude drugs that are in demand have been discovered in the Blue Ridge and Smokey mountains and people are still to be found with a knowledge of traditional herb doctoring. But Uncle Jim is ninety years old now and unable to climb up into the farthest reaches of the woods to find "sang."

His only regular source of income is $45 a month from social security. With him lives a relative, now an old lady, whom he and his wife raised from childhood. She cooks, cleans, strings shucky beans, dries apples, and tries to help with the garden and can some of the vegetables. Extremely alert for his age, Uncle Jim plants the garden and gathers wood from the mountainside, which he chops for his stove. His monthly check must take care of all their needs.

But as in any section of the United States, there are people

in Appalachia who have been fortunate, who have prospered and assumed the responsibilities of leadership in their area.

Walking down the main street of Marshall, North Carolina, past the dime store and beyond the bank, you will find a flight of stairs that leads to second-floor offices. Climb the stairs and walk to the end of the hall. Here is the door to the office of attorney and bank director Ed Mashburn. At first there is little to suggest that you have entered one of the most important rooms in Madison County. But this is typical of Appalachia. For a lawyer or a banker or, indeed, anyone to succeed here, his door must be open. "He's a mighty common man" is the local way of saying that a man mingles with others as an equal. Mountain people are quick to recognize affectation.

There is never a well-manicured secretary screening out the undesirable call. Somehow, this would be considered the height

Bank Director Ed Mashburn

of effrontery. There is no office in Marshall or, perhaps, anywhere in Appalachia that a farmer cannot walk into at ease in a pair of overalls. Although a man may be rich and able to afford modern art for his wall, a thick rug on the floor, a title on the door, and a secretary and receptionist, you won't find these outward signs of success in Appalachia. Ed Mashburn's office is as high-class as you can get in these parts without making visitors feel uncomfortable.

The windows behind his desk look over the French Broad River, which sparkles in the late afternoon sun. On the wall is a B.A. degree and a law degree from the University of North Carolina. Mashburn has a crew cut and his hair is the shade of gray that makes the crew cut acceptable. He is a warm and friendly man, a Republican and a native. He seems to typify wealth, education, and the power structure along with a genuinely progressive attitude toward his area.

Although Mashburn has played a large part in bringing industry to Madison County, he does not believe industry is the total answer to Appalachia's economic problems.

"Recreation is the most plausible way. The French Broad River will be stocked with bass. There will be recreation such as shooting the river rapids which can be developed. There will be golf courses and resorts that will provide jobs. Already, we are beginning to see people from Florida and other states coming into the county and buying land."

So, Appalachia's rugged beauty is now turning into an asset. Americans from outside this region are discovering its wonders as a vacation land. They are also finding out that behind the familiar caricature of the mountaineer there are real flesh-and-blood people who have been caught for generations within the wall of hills—a brave and uncomplaining people whose ancestry goes back to the early settlers of our nation. Appalachian leaders along with the Federal government are seeking ways to help these people experience the opportunity and abundance of life enjoyed by the rest of the nation.

3. CRAFTS ARE A FAMILY THING

"Turn down Brown Creek Road and keep going until the road gets narrower and you think it's going to end," says the man in the country store. "You'll find Wiley Blevins' house on the right."

Like Wiley Blevins, mountain craftsmen live off the main highways on dirt roads that it takes real skill and daring to drive. Junked cars are a familiar sight and the roads are one of the reasons. A car doesn't last long on rocky, rutted mountain roads, for every jolt and bump loosens bolts and abuses shock absorbers.

But chairmaker Wiley Blevins does not worry about the road being rough on cars. This warm, friendly man has never owned one for he is a deaf-mute. He is used to the long walk to the grocery store or doctor in all kinds of weather, although he sometimes rides home with a neighbor.

Each Sunday, on foot, he climbs steep, winding White Oak Creek Road to his church. Sometimes in the afternoon, after he is through working his vegetable patch, he sits on his front porch reading the large-print Bible that is one of his most prized possessions.

The rest of his time is spent working on the chairs that he makes by hand in the partial basement of his one-room home. He brought each stone himself from the creek and built the foundation. It is musty and damp but cool during the heat of the day in the little basement room where Wiley Blevins sits weaving chair bottoms from reed splits. Only a few people weave these seats for it takes time and patience.

Before he can work with the splits he plunges the bundles of reed into the icy mountain stream to soak. After a few hours they become flexible enough for him to begin weaving his chair seats. The rungs of the chair, untouched by power machinery, are still shaped on the drawhorse by hand.

Mr. Blevins makes his chairs to order or sells them at a local fair, which is held once a year. The road to his house is travelled mostly by the families who live along it so the thousands of tourists who drive by a few miles away on the main highway are not likely to learn about Wiley Blevins and his chair-making.

Since quite a few of the mountain craftsmen live off the main roads and sometimes in hard-to-find places, several of the mountain counties have formed a government-funded craft organization to help these people market their products. The craft organization has also encouraged many of the older men and women, no longer well enough to do heavy work, to take up the traditional crafts and supplement their small welfare or social security checks.

This help in selling their chairs, baskets, rugs, handmade quilts, carvings, and folk toys has given many people a fresh interest in life and a sense of pride in their newly developed skill.

In some mountain families one skill has been handed down from generation to generation. In the Hicks family it is making and playing dulcimers.

Chair-maker
Wiley Blevins

"King of the dulcimer-makers," Ed Presnell

Scarcely two months after he married Nettie Hicks, Ed Presnell made his first dulcimer. Using her father's as a model, Presnell made the dulcimer from an old poplar log. After he had made the first of these old-fashioned three-string instruments, he found such a demand for them that he kept right on. He carved them out of chestnut, sassafras, cherry, butternut, walnut, and maple, experimenting with all the different woods from the trees nearby. He would season the wood himself and polish it lovingly to bring out the grain.

For a while, Ed Presnell continued farming as he had done before he and Nettie Hicks married, and in the evening he would sit carving out his dulcimers before the fire or on the porch. As the orders began to pile up he turned entirely to dulcimer-making. He created a special design for his instruments to give them good tone quality as well as beauty. By now he has lost count of the dulcimers he has made but they number in the hundreds, and this slight, full-bearded man is now known as the "king of the dulcimer-makers." His son likes to carve animals, particularly ducks with a jaunty air and an impertinent flip to their tails. Mrs. Presnell applies the finishing touches such as sanding and polishing.

Not far from the Hicks family lives Mrs. Elsie Trivette. When she was a little girl, Mrs. Trivette watched her mother and learned how to spin. She went with her into the forest where Elsie discovered which herbs and roots produced the beautiful, soft colors for dyeing the skeins of wool.

The herbs are boiled outdoors in a huge black iron pot.

"I get my brown dyes from black walnut hulls. Some of that iron in my old pot blends in just right with the dye. Onion hulls will make yellow or orange, the sumac burrs give deep red colors, and I use polk juice to mark off the design on burlap.

"My mother taught all of us to dye and hook rugs and knot bedspreads. We supported ourselves." The wool is hooked through a burlap bag, which forms the backing for her rugs.

The organization that has done most to aid mountain craftsmen through the years is the Southern Highland Handi-

craft Guild, which has not only encouraged high standards of quality among the craftsmen but, through the Guild shops, has provided an invaluable market for mountain craft products.

One of the reasons why crafts have flourished in Appalachia is the presence of generous natural resources such as gems for the jewelry-maker, lumber for the woodcarver, clay for the potter, and honeysuckle and cane for the basket-makers. Since the mountain people are not pressed for time, they can experiment with the materials around them.

But in the frontier days and for many years after, crafts were no hobby. Skill and ingenuity with one's hands were very important to living in the wilderness. Men and women built their own houses, made their own furniture, farm implements, and clothing, and were proud of the work of their hands. The material things they made lent comfort, dignity, beauty, and recreation to their lives.

There was a sense of satisfaction simply in creating these tools and household objects, so that years later when men and women no longer had to make things, they still took pleasure in doing so. It is only natural that one of the greatest craft revivals in America is taking place in Appalachia where, until recently, craft skills were needed in daily life.

Mrs. Elsie Trivette

4. EVERY YEAR A CROP BEHIND

Asked why he grew crook-neck squash instead of pumpkins, a mountain farmer answered, "If we growed punkins up in yon cove, they'd break loose, roll down and kill somebody."

Many mountain farmers own land too steep to farm at a profit, and so it is with the Abner Wrights.

A few hundred feet up Bald Mountain Road on the right, their little house clings to the side of the mountain. Behind it is a ramshackle barn and a hogpen. Two girls about nine or ten play in the gutted-out cab of an old pickup truck that rests on the ground, its wheels long gone.

In the yard are the rusty remains of a combine, pieces of ancient cars, some scattered cement blocks, a handplow and, lying beside the house, a pile of rotted pumpkins.

Mrs. Wright, a heavy-set woman with a tanned, leathery face, answers the door and invites the visitor to "have a cheer." She is not only courteous, but has the natural unselfconscious dignity so many of the mountain people possess. Her husband and his niece Sarah have hickory split chairs pulled up to the stove for warmth and there is the odor of wood smoke from the fire.

The Wrights farm for a living. Abner Wright is fifty-nine and his wife Esther is sixty. The two little girls playing outdoors are their grandchildren.

Twenty years ago the Wrights bought this thirty-seven-acre strip of land and together they built their four-room home. That was before Abner began having stomach trouble, which has kept him from clearing as much pasture land as he would like. He and his wife look much older than their actual ages.

During the latter part of March they begin seeding their tobacco beds, covering them carefully with long lengths of white sheeting to protect the tender plants from frost. It is still cold in the mountains and some of the peaks have white streaks of snow upon them.

"Last year I wrassled with that hand plow and balky old mule to turn the furrows for my plants in this rocky, red dirt. Thirty-seven acres of land sounds purty good, but not if it goes straight up. We got rock cliffs up there so steep the cow can't even pasture. There's only about ten acres of open land we can farm."

Abner Wright gets up to push a burlap bag with his foot so that it covers the inch-high crack under the front door where the wind blows in briskly.

"And talkin' of pasture, you know what I saw the other day? That rich feller from out of state who bought the land next to us had one of them helicopters fertilizin' his pasture land. Bet that cost him aplenty!

"We always been tobacco farmers. Made $705 off it last year —that's about $2 a day, I reckon. Then they [the county agricultural committee] came along and cut us down to only half an acre. Said what we could plant depended on how much we was cultivatin' and we didn't have enough land under cultivation."

"Abner and I just ain't strong enough now to keep as much of that pasture cleared," explains Mrs. Wright. "Even if we could buy a tractor we couldn't use it on the side of this mountain. The brush, hit keeps growin' back and each year hit gits harder for us to chop it down.

"Iffen hail or freeze strikes we lose most of the crop. We had beautiful tobacco one summer. Late one evenin' I heard the hail a peltin' the roof. I could have cried, that tobacco was so tore up. We only got $45 for the whole crop that year. Then we had to go borrow. Now we owe about $2,000. We borrow to pay our food bill. We borrow to buy a few clothes. We just borrow to live. It's no wonder the young folks don't stay on the farm. They go to the cities. You can't make a livin' here."

Abner Wright nods his head. "We're a crop behind all the time."

"But we eat right well," says Mrs. Wright with pride. "I put up my own canned vegetables from the garden and we have meat about three times a week. We got the cow and two hogs, but we had to stop keepin' chickens, the neighbors faulted us so for it. The chickens kept scratchin' up their gardens and eatin' their tomatoes."

Sarah, Mr. Wright's niece, listens, sometimes smiling to herself over nothing. "We been keepin' Sarah for two years," says

Mrs. Wright. "She was always simple-minded. The welfare brought her to us two years ago. Said she couldn't take care of herself. After she got married she was livin' down the valley aways. Then her husband died an' she went to live with her daughter, but that didn't work out. Her daughter is simple, too, like Sarah."

Retardation is only one of the many problems caused by poor diet and little or no medical care.

But for a mountain family not to take in relatives who need help is unthinkable. If a woman with a shiftless husband leaves him and brings her brood of, perhaps, half a dozen children to her family, they are all taken in. The family may have only two or three rooms but she is welcomed, and at night pallets are laid on the floor.

They sell their hog—their only hope for the winter's meat and lard—to buy groceries and meat. As week follows week they use up their canned vegetables, but they will never hint that the visit may be lasting too long.

"I've always had somebody to take care of, somebody to look out for. It's milk cow, go to field, come back, fix lunch, back to field, come home of an afternoon, fix supper, hoe garden, and git to bed," says Mrs. Wright cheerfully. Although the hands in her lap are gnarled and workworn there is strength and beauty about them, too. They are more at home around a hoe than idle.

"Every fall I make a little apple butter." She smiles at the two little girls. "Maybe Cora and Sally are big enough to help me some this year." The children's eyes light up. Apologizing for the floors not being clean enough for company, she says, "The girls will let those dogs come in and 'prank' with 'em."

In the kitchen is an old iron stove with a box of wood ashes beside it. "Here is our supper," she says taking the lid from a pot. Inside is corn and tomato soup. "We had it for lunch and we'll have it again tonight with some cornbread. I try to cook once for two meals." It is hard to see how a meal like this can provide strength for heavy farm work.

A stone's throw away on a small hill is Bald Mountain Free Will Baptist Church gleaming white in the spring sunlight. Mrs. Wright is there each Sunday. "I go because I love the Lord. He's taken me through thick and thin," she says as her callused hand pulls the plastic window curtain aside and points out over the beautiful valley with purple mountain ranges rising in the distance. "You can look out on that creation and know there's a God."

The first thunderstorm of spring rumbles in the distance and Abner Wright warns about the road leading down into the valley and landslides from spring rains.

"Ever heard the story of Pete Bolin? Well, hit was rainin' hard and he'd been drivin' some calves up under the clifts when he felt the earth tremble under him. He knowed he was on a slip and he grabbed aholt of a big sugar-tree and hilt on. The whole side o' that mountain slid down trees and all.

"He went home and warmed himself by the fire a spell. Then he told his old woman. I reckon I have rid a bigger critter than you ever seen."

"You ain't been on an elephant have you, Pete?"

"No, hit warn't no elephant. I have rode four acres of land for two hundred yards."

"So, when you see one of them signs up here about a land-slide," says Mr. Wright, "remember they kin be destructious."

This land of Appalachia, which is so beautiful, is not only difficult to farm but sometimes a harsh and dangerous land in which to live.

Cloice Plemmons, the manager of Mountain Production Credit Corporation, inspects a field of burley tobacco. Created in 1932 during the Depression, the corporation made 315 loans in 1967 for a total of $1,300,000, making it an important factor in the Appalachian economy

5. THE HUNGRY ONES

The face of young Dr. Sam Jackson was white with anger as he walked down the steps of the crudely built little shack where eight people lived, ate, and slept in one room. Vester Brady and his wife had six children. Brady had sat on the bed smiling foolishly in an alcoholic stupor while each child was being checked by the doctor. He had found the four youngest boys all retarded.

"God has been so good to me today," the mother said. "For the first time Tommy tried to walk to the window and look out."

Tommy is seven years old and is still unable to walk.

"Those kids are probably retarded from malnutrition," Jackson said to his preacher friend, Reverend Turner. Listening to the preacher, the doctor had become interested enough to take a day off and go to see the children of the families Reverend Turner had been describing—children who had never been examined by a doctor in their life.

"That youngest child's going to die—the one called Tommy—either of pneumonia or the sores and infections he's getting crawling around on the floor," said Jackson bluntly.

There was no school for the retarded nearby for the other brothers. Even if there were one, there would be no transportation. The family has no car, the father no job. They live on a small monthly check from the welfare department.

Mrs. Brady, a tired-faced woman of thirty-five, never knew what it was to have a balanced diet or to be checked by a doctor during any of her pregnancies. If a public health nurse had managed to find the family and tell Mrs. Brady the importance of proper diet, she might just as well have taken one look at the family meal of corn pone (corn meal and water) baking on the old iron stove and forgotten diet. It is impossible for Mrs. Brady to make trips across the mountains of fifteen or twenty miles each way to a doctor, and even if she got there she would not be able to pay him or buy the vitamins he would recommend.

At the next house a woman in her early thirties with lanky black hair opened the door. Children spilled out of the house and began playing in the yard while Mrs. Hughes stood talking with the preacher and Dr. Jackson. The temperature outside was several degrees below freezing and Jackson noticed that Lisa, four years old and very blonde, was barefooted. He told her she ought to go indoors and get some shoes. She looked at him without answering so he spoke to her again. This time the child replied but he couldn't understand her.

"Lisa ain't got no shoes, Doc, and she don't mean nothin' by not answerin' you right off. Seems like that child just don't hear good. She's been sickly ever since she was borned."

The doctor picked up Lisa gently, took her inside, and began checking her. The little girl's hearing was so bad that she had never heard words well enough to repeat them properly. He knew only too well the reasons why. The children in this family had been either hungry or half-hungry ever since they came into the world. A poor diet meant that their bodies did not resist germs and sickness. Lisa, like many children from homes like this, had probably had continual ear infections since birth which had gradually damaged her hearing.

"But we uns are lucky, I guess," said Mrs. Hughes. "We've only had two little uns to die on us. One little girl I lost just arter she was borned and a boy when he warn't quite two."

"What did they die from, Mrs. Hughes?"

"Lawsey me, I never knowed. Can't git no doctor to come way into this holler. Just sickly I reckon."

Dr. Jackson nodded. He knew that up here children's lives came and went. There was no birth certificate to celebrate when they were born and no death certificate to mark when they died. It was as if they never really existed at all, at least not in the records of any community or county. Certainly, for all legal purposes they had never been born. He thought bitterly of the superior way Americans talked about the cheapness of human life in countries like India, and angry inside, he wondered how situations like this could exist in the United States.

Government programs such as welfare, surplus food commodities, and food stamps wait for people to come to them. It is not their policy to seek out needs or find hungry families. One Appalachian welfare commissioner says that this policy must be reversed.

"We could help twice the number of people in welfare alone if our workers were permitted to actively seek out those who are in need but don't know about available programs."

This is probably equally true of food programs. Some county commissioners have not applied for the food-stamp plan because they are unable to believe there are people in their county literally starving to death. Everyone tends to travel in his own circle of society, and because of remote, inaccessible mountain coves and hollows, poverty is far less visible in Appalachia than in a city.

One editor of a leading Tennessee paper spent fifteen years serving his community before a story which took him ten miles out of town made him realize the terrible poverty that had existed for years so close at hand. He arrived following a heavy snow at a small cabin to find the father making a stretcher from two poles and a blanket so that he could drag his pregnant

wife down the side of the mountain when her labor pains began.

He planned to pull her to the old family car which had no gears and was going to let it roll down the mountain to the road where he hoped to get a passing car to take his wife to the hospital. They had no telephone and no close neighbors.

Out in the front yard stood a grotesque old white bathtub which the family used to bathe in when it was warm enough in the summer. All the water for the house had to be carried in empty Clorox jugs from a nearby stream, and the woods at the back of the house was the family bathroom.

"Ten minutes from my home, but a world away, I met this family," says the newspaper editor.

"Cleanliness seems fruitless to them—perhaps they don't try, perhaps they don't know how or understand the need. They want a warmer place for the winter but the father was injured on his last job and who wants to rent to a nonproductive family? They're not bitter, or jealous, just hopeless. They ask for nothing—but they seem to be waiting for some sort of miracle to release them from the situation in which they're caught."

There are almost no poor Negro families to be found in situations like this in rural Appalachia (probably because they have not settled there) with the exception of the mountainous areas of Georgia and Alabama. Half of all the black people of Appalachia are concentrated in this southernmost tip.

In many Appalachian counties there may be no more than a handful of Negro families. Jobs are scarce, so blacks seek out cities like Chattanooga, Tennessee, and Charleston, South Carolina, or the coal mining area of McDowell County, West Virginia, where employment opportunities are greater.

6. HILL COUNTRY CUSTOMS

Eleven-year-old Frieda Hicks wakes with a pleasurable sense of excitement. She knows today is a very special day.

Her oldest sister, Ruth, is here from Florida and her oldest brother, Bobby Joe, who has been away at school in Tennessee, is also at home for Decoration Sunday.

She splashes water on her round, freckled face and dresses quickly to go downstairs. Right after breakfast, she and her younger brother, Billy, will go out back of the house to the banks of Cranberry Creek and pick armloads of wildflowers.

Decoration Sunday is an important event for the Hicks and for many other mountain families. Each year on the fourth Sunday of July, sons, daughters, and relatives who have scattered far and wide seeking better opportunities all come home. They help gather the unbelievably beautiful giant dahlias, the pride of so many mountain housewives, along with shasta daisies and native wildflowers, and carry them to the cemetery to decorate the family graves.

It's a time of reunion and visiting for those who now live far away. Perhaps it is sentiment, perhaps it is an excuse to escape the crowds and heat of the concrete city which brings them home to the cool refreshment of the mountains.

"Why do we always go on the fourth Sunday? Because that's the day the old folks always went," says Mrs. Hicks.

After lunch she brushes Frieda's red-gold hair before the mirror of the big oak dresser in the sitting room. Bobby Joe has picked up his girl and now the family is ready to leave. Billy and Frieda race to get in the family car, their older sisters following more sedately. Bobby Joe looks at the family car full of children and flowers and explains to his father that he will follow with his girl friend in his own car.

Driving over to the nearby town of Elk Park, Mr. Hicks turns down Elk River Road and, a short distance from town, pulls over and parks along the shoulder of the road beside the river. From this point the trip to the cemetery must be made on foot. Single file they follow a narrow path fringed with tall brush. Now and then blackberry briars scratch Frieda's bare legs. The

path leads to a shallow ford on the Elk River where a huge oak tree has been felled to bridge the water. Foot-logs are still used over many mountain streams and this one is the customary way for visitors to the cemetery to cross the river. Frieda and Billy run across the big log laughing at the sport of it. Billy almost loses his balance but recovers it just in time. The grown-ups carrying the flowers walk more carefully but with surprising assurance. The rickety rail of boards supported by tree branches forms a precarious support.

At the end of the path is a pasture gate which Albert Hicks holds open, closing it after everyone has passed through. The Hicks are joined here by friends who are also on their way to the cemetery. Now, children and older people alike begin to climb the narrow road, really more of a trail, which curves around the side of the mountain. Frieda and Billy are already way ahead of the grown-ups. Bobby Joe and his girl, arms around each other's waist, are in no hurry.

"Only a jeep can go up this road to the top," says Mrs. Hicks, "and in bad weather the men have to carry the casket. A jeep can't get up here if there's been too much snow."

It's a climb that leaves a lowlander breathless, but the Hicks take it for granted. Finally they come out of the forest at the very crest of the mountain. Before them lies a lush green meadow dotted with white markers.

Even the old people have managed to make their way across the foot-log and up the mountain. One of them says, "Folks would be a lot better off if they'd look up to the hills more often. There's help and strength there just like the Bible says."

Mr. and Mrs. Hicks walk over to the graves of their parents with Frieda and Billy following. Bobby Joe and his girl are at the edge of the cemetery looking out over the valley below. With the children helping, the flowers are arranged on the graves. Mrs. Hicks has brought a jar of water which she pours into the small glass jars sunk in the earth at the head of each grave. She thrusts the evergreen branches into the earth still moist from the rain of the night before. The dahlias and wildflowers go into the jars she has filled with water.

Even the children become quieter and more thoughtful than usual. After they finish arranging the flowers and greenery, Albert Hicks stops in front of his grandfather's grave, leaning forward to read the weatherworn letters and pointing them out to the children. But Frieda and Billy are impatient to go and Bobby Joe and his girl are already on their way back down the steep little mountain road.

Albert and Lucy Mae Hicks pause for a silent moment together as they look out over the valleys and ridges stretching off into the distance. They are probably the only members of the family who are thinking that someday their own children will stand here in their place.

Why would anyone put a graveyard on the very top of a mountain difficult to reach even by jeep and a struggle to climb on foot? Perhaps the early settlers felt that in death as in life they would want to look out over their beloved mountains. They may also have thought of loved ones who, year after year, would climb these heights until they were short of breath and their legs weak under them, but whose spirits would soar as they looked at the beauty of the distant ranges.

So, mountain ways have never been city ways and hill country customs and sayings are strange to city folk. Perhaps this is because the life of mountain people is tied much more closely to the weather, the phases of the moon, and the gifts of the land.

Farmers watch the moon for the right time to plant. Crops that bear their fruit above ground must be planted when the moon is full. Those that produce underground like turnips, potatoes, and onions must be planted only during the days when the moon has waned to its darkest point. Trees, too, must be cut at the dark of the moon so that the stumps will rot rather than sprout again. Shingles and boards are sure to warp if they are not hammered down when the tip of the new moon points earthward.

The ancient art of soap-making can take place only on a waning moon or the soap is "sartin to boil over." Its secrets are passed on from mother to daughter and this household skill is still practiced by a surprising number of mountain women. In the early days hickory ashes were carefully saved from the fireplace. Water was poured on the ashes and the drippings caught in a container. Bits of pork skin were cooked slowly until the grease from them was rendered. Lye water from the ashes and the grease were boiled together in a huge iron pot out in the yard.

Now, commercial lye is used rather than the water from wood ashes but the method is still the same. Housewives use a sassafras stick to stir the boiling soap and the stick contributes some of its own spicy, pungent odor. When the sassafras bark falls off it's a sign the soap is ready.

The snowy-white liquid is dipped from the iron pot into jars or a long, flat box to harden. Women who make it say "It's a powerful good cleaner and better'n any store-bought soap."

One of the customs children look forward to eagerly is apple-butter making. In the early fall the apple trees on the mountain sides are so laden with delicious fruit that they most resemble Christmas trees hung with bright red balls.

This is the time of year Mrs. Decie Singleton begins her ritual of making apple butter and nothing could smell or taste any better. She selects the choicest apples and spends hours sitting on the back steps with a bowl in her lap peeling them. Her husband, Andy, carves out a long wooden stirring paddle holding it between his knees to shape and smooth it.

While the morning dew is still glistening on the grass, the apples are placed in an iron pot over a fire and a jug of fresh-made cider poured over them. Decie begins to stir slowly and rhythmically. Andy tends the fire, occasionally adding a log while smoke curls up around the pot. It is a daylong process and not for the lazy. If the apples are not continually stirred they will stick and burn. Decie's strong, spare body bends tirelessly over the pot. When fragrant steam rises and the apples begin to bubble, she adds sugar and spices.

As the apple butter thickens, it takes on a rich brownish-red color and becomes harder to stir. The afternoon wears on and the sun drops lower in the sky. By now there is a crispness in the air and a breeze ruffles the trees. At last the butter is thick enough to pour and Andy must sample it smacking his lips appreciatively. With pothooks he lifts the heavy black pot from the wood embers.

Another batch of tasty apple butter is ready for the long winter months, and the ritual will not be repeated until next fall when the sumac leaves turn flaming red along the roadsides and the sassafras trees are a golden glow.

Just as mountain customs are tied to the turn of the seasons, the sayings have grown out of a close association with nature. Although many quaint expressions are dying out because of radio and television, you may still hear some of them if you leave the beaten path and explore the high reaches of the mountains where the tall, dark balsams grow.

These are words and phrases that might have come right out of Chaucer or Shakespeare—*hit* (for *it*), *holp* (for *help*), *beastes* (for *beasts*), *poke* (for a *bag*), *mought* (for *might*), *agin* (for *again*) and *yander* (for *yonder*). People who have been far from the sea for over two hundred years may call their sweetheart

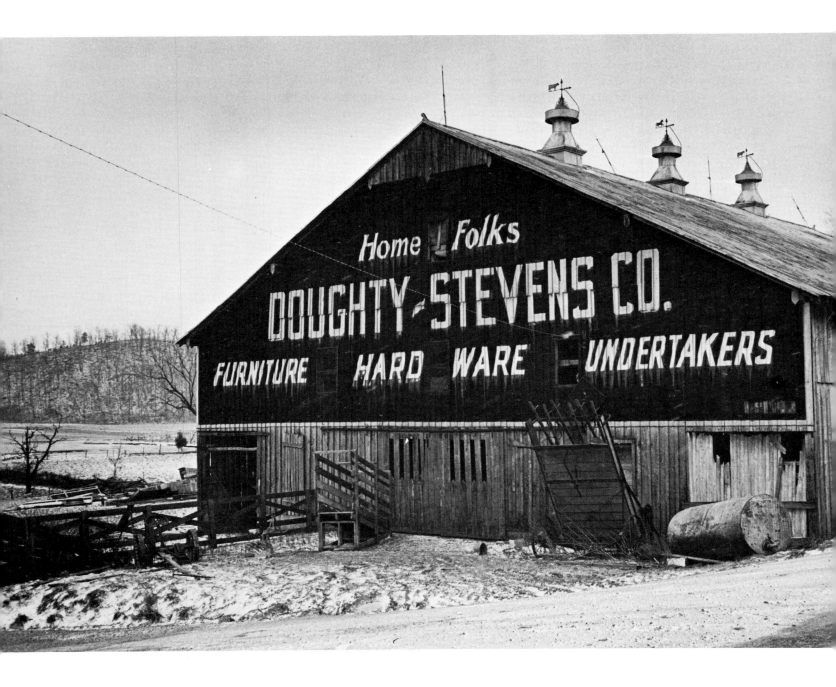

"doney gal," an expression used by British sailors. Beans that have been dried in the pod and strung are called "leather-britches" and apple sauce is called "sass."

A mountain man doesn't throw a stone, he "flings a rock," and a fellow who leaves in a hurry has "lit a shuck for home." If you ask a mountaineer how he feels, he may reply "middlin" or "fair to middlin," which means he could feel better.

The rivers, the gorges, the streams were all named for some event that took place there. Stillhouse Branch was once the hideout of moonshiners. Calf-killer Run is where a marauding bear once roamed. Appalachia has had its share of violence reflected in names like Squabble, Gouge-eye, Shooting Creek, Vengeance, and Hell Mountain.

Hardships were part of life and from them came names like Long Hungry, Bone Valley, Poor Fork, Needmore, Weary Hut, and Broken Leg. But a rough sort of humor also prevailed and there are names like Chunky Gal, Shake a Rag, and Squeeze Betsy, which is a narrow passage between two cliffs.

People looked up at the mountains and named them after whatever they thought they resembled. There are mountains called Hogback, Hound Ears, Standing Indian, The Devil's Courthouse, Sharp Top, and Naked Place.

Typical of the sayings are: "Sap-risin' time is lovin' time," "Don't neglect your own field to plant your neighbor's," "The sun is the poor man's clock," "If the sun shines when it's rainin' the devil's beatin' his wife," and "Don't hist one foot until the other's settin' flat."

There is a wealth of meaning in the comment "Our folks got naturalized to the doctor and like him." Or, where a road has been gutted out by rain, "You'll have to surround it." Richly descriptive, mountain speech is often unhampered by grammar, and thus it may have a fresh quality that captures the thought of the moment before it takes flight. Nor do the people hesitate to make words or phrases to fit the occasion—a rare quality.

7. RECREATION MOUNTAIN STYLE

Cindy got religion, had it once before,
When she heard my banjo,
She 'uz first one on the floor.

The young folks aren't the only ones who can't keep their feet
still when that swinging tune about a gal named Cindy starts up.
You don't meet many people in the mountains who can't saw
a fiddle or twang a banjo. And when three or four get together
around the fireside at night, there are fiddle tunes that set even
the old folks' feet remembering.

In a semi-dark room with firelight dancing on the walls, someone will start to sing softly and others will join in. The old songs
and ballads tell stories about real people and real events, of
courtship and marriage, unrequited love or the faithless maid,
and usually, before the night is over, of "darling Cora," the
swashbuckling mountain heroine, whose affections were not to
be taken lightly for she wore a .44!

One of the most famous banjo ballads was written about the
beautiful young girl, Kidder Cole. While a rival danced the night
away with Kidder, her heartbroken lover began composing his
ballad. One of the verses goes:

If I ever have a fight
I hope it will be with Charley Wright
For he was the ruin of my soul
When he beat my time with Kidder Cole.

There was once a day when every mountain community had
its street singers or balladeers. This was often the way news
travelled since there was no radio and most people seldom saw
a paper. One of the most famous of the old time balladeers is
the man they call the Minstrel of the Appalachians, Bascom
Lamar Lunsford, who roamed the mountains for years, visiting
old timers, urging them to play their tunes with him, singing,
playing, and dancing as he went. Now in his eighties, he is a
living storehouse of the traditional music.

Banjo-maker and player Tab Ward

Collectors have long realized that Madison County in western North Carolina near the Tennessee line is a rich source for folk music that has been handed down orally for generations. Mountain folk festivals held in Asheville, North Carolina, and in Berea, Kentucky, stimulate interest in folk culture. At such festivals, mountain children and grown-ups do smooth square dancing and clog dancing (similar to the Irish Jig) to the tune of the guitar, banjo, and dulcimer. This music comes from the jigs and reels of England and Scotland.

But outside of a family reunion, people back in the hill country aren't in the habit of planning social events just for fun. To find themselves at the kind of cocktail party many couples attend in the world outside of Appalachia would probably give a mountain man and his wife "the allovers"—a mountain term for nervousness.

"Recreation" even today is mostly socializing. It may take

place at an event like molasses-making, which has a fall festival quality for mountain folk. Corn-shucking, bean-stringing, and molasses-making may all be occasions for fun while serving an economic need, too. The corn is used for feed or ground into meal to be eaten in corn bread; the dried beans are strung in late summer to be brought out during the winter months; and the "long sweetenin'" (molasses syrup) is sopped up on corn bread or hot biscuits.

A golden autumn day before frost comes finds Colby Powell and his neighbor cutting their cane to make molasses. If they let the frost strike before they get their crop out of the field, the cane is ruined and the juice will turn sour.

Sorghum grows much like corn and is tended like corn, but the top of the stalk bears a tall spike of reddish-colored seeds. The cane is cut, gathered in bundles, and taken to the cane mill where it is forced through a crusher. Colby carefully feeds the

stalks in and Jake Robertson pulls them through. A horse is hitched to a pole secured to the center of the crusher, and, by walking round and round in a circle, furnishes the power to turn the two cogged wheels that crush the cane.

The juice, at first pale green, is poured into a long, shallow trough and cooked. It must be stirred constantly and the greenish foam skimmed off the top. The men take turns stirring and stoking the wood fire beneath the trough. It's an all-day job, but there is time to swap tales and visit as the smell of cooking syrup mingled with hickory smoke rises in the air.

Children scamper up to peer over the edge of the trough at the bubbling syrup. By the end of the afternoon the amber liquid is ready to taste and pour into the long row of jars. Eager young hands scrape the sweet white foam from the trough with sticks and eat all they can hold.

Nobody has ever written down a recipe for making molasses and nobody goes by a clock.

"A man's just got to have a feel for it and know when it's ready."

Passed down from father to son, it is an art that takes a long time to learn. There is no similarity between the "store-bought" product and the delicate flavor of real mountain-made molasses.

8. MOUNTAIN BOOTLEGGERS MEAN BUSINESS

It was late at night and the preacher had just finished a two-hour sermon in a rugged area near Trap Hill, North Carolina. He was to spend the night at a mountain cabin, and his host accompanied him in the preacher's old car as it lurched crazily along over the bumps and holes of the rough dirt road.

Suddenly he and his companion saw a dozen or more men jump from the bushes beside the road about fifty feet ahead. The men brandished huge sticks, and the preacher was about to stop when his host exclaimed, "Don't stop now, whatever you do. Step on the gas and give this old car all it will take. We're going to have to go right through that crowd for they're aimin' to kill you. I don't believe if you hit 'em the law will hold you guilty."

The parson had just delivered a fiery sermon in the heart of moonshine country on the evils of making corn liquor, and the moonshiners were filled with wrath.

The preacher stepped hard on the accelerator. The car seemed to pause for a suspense-filled moment, as if gathering all the power it could muster, then plunged ahead through the crowd while sticks battered it and stones crashed against the windows.

The crowd parted as the old car catapulted through it, and a short while later the two men pulled up to the small cabin where the preacher was to spend the night with his friend. The pair emerged still shaken by their close call but with only a broken rear window to show for it.

A stranger who wanders off the main road into a bootlegging area is going to be looked over carefully. In fact, eyes from the top of some ridge may be watching him every foot of the way. If he stops at a store for directions, the storekeeper may first ask, "What business you got up on the mountain?" Behind his probing eyes he is probably wondering if the visitor has come to make trouble.

Turning off the highway, driving up a mountain road that ends abruptly, and then scrambling down the side of the mountain on foot into a hollow occupied by a few shacks may lead to an eerie experience.

This happened to one traveller who approached a house where he saw smoke drifting from the stone chimney. As he got closer a small boy ran from a woodshed and in the back door of the house, slamming it behind him.

The man stepped gingerly on the rotting boards of the front steps and knocked on the door. There was the tiniest movement of the curtains at the window, and he was certain someone was peeping through at him. In fact, he began to sense that he was being watched through those curtains by several people.

No one ever answered although he knocked repeatedly. As he walked back up the hill, he still had the strange feeling he was being observed intently, almost as if he were an animal being tracked down. Standing perfectly still, he peered into the woods. With a start he detected a movement from behind a tree. Gradually, he began to make out the outline of a man's head. The body was concealed by the tree trunk. Extremely frightened, he ran toward his car as fast as he could and drove off.

The lost traveller was lucky. He might have found himself looking down the barrel of a shotgun with a mountain tough on the other end who would make some of the characters out of Dodge City appear to be real gentlemen. He had probably encountered a bootlegger with a still close by. In a case like this "foreigners" aren't welcome. The stills are often hidden way up under a cliff near a spring. They are protected by impenetrable thickets, and a revenuer can risk his life trying to crawl through one of these dense "laurel hells."

These people don't do much socializing with outsiders. Their world is one of hardship, ignorance, and intermarriage with relatives in the same cove or hollow. In many of these naturally isolated hollows it is not unusual for almost all the families to have the same last name. They are ever on the alert for the sheriff or revenue officers. Murder isn't always discovered as no one is eager to call in the law.

Census takers along with the organized church are unaware of these people's very existence. School for the children is regarded casually by parents who have no particular ambition for their youngster's future other than the life they have always known themselves.

Land that has not been fertilized for years gets farmed out, and there is easier money to be made from corn liquor. The fathers make it, while sons and grandsons grow up helping and watching the yellow-white liquid flow through the copper coil of the still. Good corn liquor is almost colorless and tasteless. This is why it is called "white lightning." The effect is like drinking pure alcohol.

As far back as pioneer days, stilling became a way of life for some mountaineers and much of their socializing and hospitality centered around it. The old-time mountain preachers, themselves a product of frontier life, did not hate whiskey or preach against its evils. In fact a fruit jar of corn whiskey was sometimes placed close at hand so that they might quench their thirst during the lengthy sermons. It is still not uncommon for a drunk to distract the other worshipers or for a delivery of whiskey to change hands behind the church.

Bootleggers even advertise if you know the signs to look for. Often it is a part of a bush or twig apparently cut off casually with a pocket knife and then dropped in the path. Many a thirsty man has taken the direction in which the stem points, following a number of them until he reaches the still.

Since many mountaineers keep shotguns for hunting or warding off predatory animals, there is sometimes a killing when the drinking gets heavy.

"Hit used to be," says a judge, "that when a man killed another all his friends rushed in and went on his bail, but now the sympathy's all with the corpse."

But for years making whiskey was not illegal, and stills provided the main source of income for some families. Laws passed in Washington were considered not only ridiculous but unfair. Old moonshiners have been heard to remark: "I raised this corn, I got a right to eat it, I got a right to drink it, and dern the man that says I can't sell it if a fellow wants to buy it."

Saturday afternoon is frequently delivery day, and it is not

*Reverend Charles Keyes,
better known as the "Parson
of the Hills," has waged a
battle against moonshine for
many years as he made the
rounds among his "chicken
coop churches" like this one*

uncommon to meet a car careening around the hairpin curve of a dirt road enveloped in a cloud of dust. A bootlegger with a load of white lightning is not going to travel slowly enough for an approaching car to see him well, much less stop him.

One of the popular sports in the southeast is stock-car racing, and some of the well-known stock-car drivers are from the mountains. In fact, some drivers used to get their racing experience running illegal whiskey.

Making her rounds in her yellow jeep, Anna Fox is a familiar and welcome sight to the families who lead isolated lives back in the hill country of rugged Madison County. Here the mountains are crowded so close together that there is little level land. Their beauty will take your breath away, but so will some of the roads, for the valleys are deeper, the hills steeper, and the edge of the road seems to drop off more precipitously than in almost any other section of the United States.

Mrs. Fox is a public-health nurse and the problems she talks over with the families she calls upon may range from bedbugs to those of lonely, elderly people or the mentally ill.

A sturdy little woman with cropped dark hair, she can be very resourceful when circumstances require it. She faces unexpected adventures on her rounds through rough country with the same quiet courage and independence characteristic of the mountain people she visits. Sometimes the road before her may be partly blocked by a landslide. Anna Fox shifts her jeep into low and goes over it. If a tree felled by an ice storm lies across the road, she may have to take off through the underbrush and circle it, and many is the time the little yellow jeep churns through small streams that nobody ever thought worthy of a bridge.

The county she serves is not a wealthy one, but Madison leaders have successfully sought federal, state, and local funds to attack Appalachian health problems. With this backing, Anna Fox brings advice and nursing care to the sick, encourages many people to take tuberculosis tests, arranges for surgery when it is needed, and refers others to eye clinics or public-health physicians. Doctors in private practice can hardly afford to bring this kind of care to widely scattered mountain families.

A day spent making calls on patients, with each call ten or fifteen miles apart over winding mountain roads, not only consumes a great deal of time but is also expensive. Many of the doctor's patients may be small farmers or families on welfare who are able to pay only the most modest fee. Sometimes they

Mrs. Anna Fox

put off calling a doctor when they need one because they are not able to pay him, so disease goes too long without proper treatment or any treatment at all.

The "granny woman" (mid-wife) still delivers many a baby. And rural mothers are seldom under a doctor's care either before or during childbirth. It's not surprising that most recorded infant deaths occur within two weeks after birth.

Mrs. Fox and her co-worker, Mrs. Naomi Garrison, a child-health nurse, regularly visit almost two hundred patients at home. About half of them have heart disease. The rest are children suffering from either rheumatic fever or diabetes.

It is impossible to bring all the many kinds of medical treatment to a patient's home, so Mrs. Fox brings the patient to a county health clinic. The clinics she has organized include maternity care, child health, X ray, immunization shots, and eye examinations. A clinic is usually staffed by a doctor two days a month. Hopefully, the number of days can be increased; however, some counties in Appalachia have no doctor at all staffing clinics, for there just aren't enough doctors to go around. More public-health nurses are also needed, for without adequate staff a health department can only report contagious diseases and life statistics of births and deaths.

Because the poor never have the money for proper diet and good medical care, there is always more sickness among them. When a public-health nurse enters a home where there is overwhelming poverty, she often finds bad sanitation and ignorance of how germs are spread.

Even when a house is kept scrupulously clean, there is sometimes little knowledge of sanitary cleanliness or disinfectants. Homes may be overcrowded. The sick and the well sleep together using the same dipper or glass to drink from and the same towel.

Neighbors arrive to show sympathy and sit with a bedridden person by the hour while a contagious illness goes unrecognized. Waste is thrown or left to seep into a nearby stream to be

carried along to a family lower down the mountain. The drinking water comes from a spring or a well and whether it has ever been tested or not, it is considered safe to drink if it sparkles cold and clear. "Hit bubbles right out o' the ground, hit's bound to be pure."

Some counties in Appalachia less progressive than Madison have scarcely made a start toward solving the health problems of their area.

"The most incredible, most stunning experience I ever had happened to me when I first came here to work," says Jean Gilliam. A young woman with short, curly blonde hair, Miss Gilliam is a nutritionist employed by the Appalachian Regional Health Council. Her stupendous task was to take the thousands of people scattered over the four-county area to which she was assigned and teach them how to serve their families healthful food.

This meant not only a staggering amount of travel but the knack of making suggestions in a friendly, tactful manner so that a mountain woman would change her ideas of a lifetime about eating and cooking and serve her family a much wider variety of food. The traditional steady diet of corn and pork, if not supplemented, can mean less energy and poor health.

In order to learn her way around, Miss Gilliam went out at first with public-health nurses on their rounds. At one rural home where she stopped to talk about dental care for a child in school, the mother began talking about one of her problems.

She pointed to a frail little girl about three. "Joannie had so much trouble breathin' awhile back, it gave me a real fright. I tried reachin' down into the back of her throat an' you know, I just scraped out gobs and gobs of worms."

Jean Gilliam was horrified. "I've read about these things in textbooks, but I couldn't believe you'd find it once in this country anywhere."

This is an extreme case, but a home that is "unbelievably dirty" like the one this little girl lived in is a breeding ground for worms. Many Appalachian children, although not this badly infested, could be given worm medicine almost routinely.

But even the public-health nurses are unable to visit all who need help. Throughout Appalachia, down in the coves, back in the hollows, and along the creek beds, live thousands of people our society doesn't even know exist.

Mrs. Fox comforts a boy who will soon go into the hospital for an eye operation

"Danny, Dannee, Dannee-e-e!"

Danny Hall crawls reluctantly out from beneath a huge pile of quilts leaving his two little brothers still in bed asleep. The linoleum floor is icy cold under his bare feet. In the early morning darkness his hand searches the chair next to his bed for his pants and shirt.

It is almost six o'clock and time for Danny to feed the chickens, the mule, and the cow. Later his mother will feed the two hogs. He stops long enough in the barn to play with the silky, brown puppies that tumble around his feet nipping joyfully at the frayed cuffs of his blue jeans.

"Danny, you take too much time out there playin' with them dogs," says his mother. "Take this basin and water out on the back porch and wash yer face. Then sit right down and eat some breakfast. That bus is agoin' to be here any minute.

"You've already missed gittin' your report card twicet for bein' absent so much."

"Well, Mama, that ain't my fault if the bus can't git up here an' you won't let me walk down to the road."

"Walk three miles down to the road and hit plumb dark out? No, I'm not agoin' to let you walk. You'd have to carry a lantern and you're still liable to get bit by a snake or some varmint. I worry enuf every day 'bout you goin' clean off the mountain in that bus."

"Oh, mama, hit ain't never gone off the road yet."

The toot of a horn sounds out front and the headlights of a bus stare out of the blackness like two bright eyes. Danny shakes the fine dark hair back from his forehead, gives his mother a quick hug around the waist, and dashes out the door.

The bus is orange like most school buses but much shorter and smaller. It is far from new. The state has told the school, "Don't ever take one of our big school buses up that road. You'll lose it!" So Danny's bus is a little one that the county sends up to his house.

When Danny gets in he sits down on one of the two long seats which run the length of the bus on each side. They are covered

*The Hicks children are fortunate in living on a
paved road. Their school bus has already climbed
dirt roads to pick up others who live on the hilltops*

with dusty, worn tan leather. Danny sits right behind the bus driver. The road is frozen and not slippery this morning, but the ruts are bad after the winter's snow, and Danny holds tightly to the back of the driver's seat. It may be that the mid-day sun will thaw the ruts, and if the road is too muddy and slippery for the bus to drive that afternoon, Danny will have to walk up the mountain to his house.

Jake Bromley, who drives the bus to the top of Wildcat Mountain to pick up Danny and his two cousins, is in high school. He is always in a good humor and never acts worried even when the going is rough as it is today. Sometimes it seems to Danny that the bus is headed straight down! He doesn't like to look over at "that purty view" his dad sometimes points out.

Danny's stomach always feels better when he tries not to notice that right beside the wheels there is nothing but blue air and a sharp drop hundreds of feet down to Rocky Creek winding along at the foot of Wildcat Mountain. It takes his breath away and reminds him of how he wakes up at night sometimes barely able to breathe. His mama calls that asthma.

Jake Bromley blows the horn about three times before the little bus inches slowly around each looping curve. He can't see whether anything is coming from the other side. The road is wide enough for only one vehicle and so steep it must be a jeep like his daddy's or have five gears like the little orange school bus. A car can't get up Wildcat Mountain.

The bus shakes, jolts, and quivers. Danny knows it must be starting through one of the small streams that run across the road. The state doesn't allow its buses to drive through streams because it is bad for the brakes.

About 8:15, over an hour after Danny leaves home, the bus pulls up in front of a brown-rock school building in western North Carolina. Stones from the mountains and streams have been fitted together carefully to build schools, fine homes, and many a cabin chimney throughout Appalachia.

Before pulling open the heavy door of the school, Danny stops for a minute to listen to the tune of the stream and inhale the fresh, cool air. Then the familiar odor of school and classrooms envelops him. The murmur of children's voices echoes from the rooms with their high ceilings. The plaster in the hall is cracked here and there. Floors are uneven, many of the boards warped. Both rooms and hall might be more cheerful if fresh, bright paint obliterated forever the old shades of green.

Morning sunlight streams through the tall windows of Danny's classroom. The janitor seldom looks high enough to sweep out the strands of cobweb in the window corners or along the edges of the ceiling. The windows are slightly raised and in between Mrs. Morgan's instructions Danny can hear the voice of the stream. She is passing out some patterns for the children in her combined third and fourth grade to color. Few schools in Appalachia have special teachers for art or music or physical education. Exercise is something the children are supposed to get enough of at home.

Danny's favorite room in the whole school is the attractive new library. A few years ago there was no library room, only a confusion of dilapidated books stacked high in the classroom cupboard. Some had pages missing and many had no title at all on the black tape along the back of the book. So, Danny never knew at first glance whether he was picking up a silly old girl's book or the good kind about animals and pioneer days.

The library Danny likes so well is not paid for out of the school budget. Most of the new books have been bought with money from ESEA (Elementary School Education Act). This money from the federal government has provided libraries for many schools in Appalachia that otherwise could never have afforded them.

Madison County in western North Carolina uses ESEA money not only to provide fine libraries for each school, but also to give daily help to children with reading problems. The same money buys power tools to train the boys and typewriters for business courses, and pays the salary of a registered nurse to check the children for health problems that may be causing learning problems.

No one knows how long youngsters like Danny will have up-to-date reference books or daily help to improve their reading, for each year Congress cuts down ESEA money for Appalachia. Fighting wars is expensive and there is seldom enough money to buy both books and bombs.

Recently, the ESEA director of Madison County invited a friend from the state capital to see the library at the Marshall school.

"I told the fellow from the State Department of Education that when he got in Marshall to just drive onto the bridge over the river and turn right when he got to the middle of it. That man thought I was telling him to go jump in the lake or something! He didn't know that our school in Marshall is on an island in the middle of the French Broad River."

School Superintendent
Robert Edwards

A couple of blocks from the "school on an island" is the "hottest seat" in Madison County. At least this is the way County School Superintendent Robert Edwards describes his chair in the superintendent's office at the beautiful old county court-house. Edwards has cropped brown hair, a smooth, unlined face and in his well-tailored, dark-green suit he would look perfectly at home in any executive gathering. But beneath his easy-going, pleasant manner lie strong determination and energy. Clasping his hands behind his head, Edwards leans back in the "hot seat" and talks about some of the inner workings of the county schools which, over the years, have been the source of more talk, conflict, accusations, pride, hope, and frustration than any subject but politics.

A few years ago the decision was made to consolidate one outlying school with the Marshall High School. The parents were proud of "their own school" and were angry when told their boys and girls would have to ride the bus six miles to the Marshall High School.

When the school buses arrived on the appointed morning to take the children to the Marshall school, they were greeted by some well-armed parents carrying pistols and knives. It is hard for a bus driver to explain the advantages of consolidation when parents are in this frame of mind! The buses went back to town empty.

Roads are steep and curvy, and there are cliffs the bus can slide off in winter when the roads are slippery with ice. So it is more than a matter of pride with these parents. They are concerned about their children's safety.

"Consolidation is opposed by nature and by human nature conspiring and combining in a way that makes an educator want to tear his hair, jump out the window, and run until he comes to some flat land!" says Edwards.

"Up here in the mountains our school buses drive twenty-eight hundred miles every day. This is like driving forty kids to California every morning, only we have to do it not on good highways or in good weather but on the crookedest, up and down roads you ever saw; some of them unpaved and some one-way."

Why is consolidation necessary? Edwards points to the large map on the wall of his office. "Here is a school up in a cove. It's got eighty-five students and the state allows us three teachers for it. The kids are in eight different grades. Those three teachers have got to teach English, arithmetic, history, social studies, science, and home economics on eight different levels. It's impossible, so you have to concentrate most on basic subjects like English or arithmetic. A boy at one school ended up having to take home economics because it was the only class available, so he sat in a high-school class of girls who were learning how to cook and sew!"

"Last year 24 percent of our graduates went on to college. Obviously, they need a college preparatory curriculum, but we have other students we know aren't going to college who should be offered a variety of vocational courses. There are all sorts of jobs we could help train them for if we can find out their talents. We've also got to help and encourage kids who don't know what they want to do yet. This can't be done in a little four-room school out there in the hills where the principal needs to spend most of the day teaching classes."

"I have to speak several languages," says Edwards. "I must talk to the man in the cabin down on the cliff whose father and grandfather, as well as himself, thought seventh grade was as far as anyone needed to go and I've got to tell him it's the law their kids go to school through the twelfth grade. I have to talk to the well-educated merchant and professional man in Marshall or the college instructor over at Mars Hill who complains because he wants the best possible preparatory course for his kid who is going to college."

Edwards is proud of his teachers, sixteen of whom have master's degrees, but frustrated because, he says, "I don't get one-third of the money our schools need when I ask for it."

Most of the schools were built in the twenties, with a few minor additions since, but a new school has not been built in thirty years. County politicians have wanted to keep the debt down.

"The debt is down to practically nothing, but at the same time, we've built nothing, created nothing."

Bob Edwards' problems are similar to those of many other school superintendents in Appalachia. Even educational television has been slow to reach the children because the mountains are natural barriers to good reception.

The answer to these obstacles, says Edwards, is money. Money and good roads. Whose money? "Anybody's money," he replies. "We can do it with anybody's money."

What is he going to do about the situation?

"I'm going to be a duck. You know a duck keeps his feathers in order above water and is calm and serene. I try to be like that duck but underneath the water, I am paddling like hell to change things!"

Appalachian schoolchildren
enjoy their folksongs

11. POLITICAL DYNAMITE

Zeno Ponder is probably one of Appalachia's most colorful political figures. He has been both praised and damned, appointed to high positions, and had sticks of dynamite thrown into his yard!

Politics has never been dull in mountainous Madison County. Nor is there anything boring about Mr. Ponder's career, which has made news in most of the state papers and reverberated all the way to the governor's mansion.

"I'm no political boss and I don't think people should call me one," says ruddy-faced, friendly Zeno Ponder. "I guess you would say I'm a politician interested in helping this county get ahead."

Mr. Ponder's comfortable, attractive home is perched on top of a hill near Marshall, North Carolina. Chewing on a blade of grass he leans against the white fence and looks thoughtfully out over the green hills of his well-kept dairy farm. He enjoys farming and he also enjoys politics.

"You know, people up here take their politics pretty serious and arguments between Republicans and Democrats sometimes used to be settled with bullets rather than ballots.

"But you've got to understand why people feel so bitter." The tall redheaded man's eyes seem unconscious of the present as if they are looking far back into the past, but a past still very real to him.

Western North Carolina as well as Tennessee, Kentucky, and a big part of Appalachia had many Union sympathizers during the Civil War. These families had little in common with plantation owners farther south. After the war those who had sympathized with the Union became Republicans and the families that had sided with the Confederacy became Democrats. During the war both armies had raided the area and lifelong friends became suspicious of each other. This disagreement over the war left distrust and hatred among many mountain families and led to long, bloody feuds. Children grew up hearing their parents talk of their hatred for another family and they passed it along to their own children. Emotions spawned years ago bred bitterness that still exists between some members of both political parties.

"This county was always carried by the Republicans," says Ponder, "and in our state the legislature is almost one hundred percent Democrat. They knew the Democratic party would never get any votes up here so when we asked for money to build roads or anything else, they didn't pay much attention. They gave funds to the counties which had voted for them and supported them. So control by one party has hurt us on both the state and county level."

After he was graduated from college and served in the army during World War II, Zeno Ponder, with only a handful of supporters, set out to build a Democratic party. The opposition might call it a "machine" but Ponder doesn't think of it that way.

"The Republican party had a stranglehold on this county and I set out to break it."

His first act was to try and convince the group of veterans he was teaching that two parties rather than one were essential if the legislature was ever going to give Madison money for roads and other projects.

Politician Zeno Ponder

Marshall,
North Carolina

"I felt Madison County was out of step with the times. Many of the fellows [700 veterans] who had returned to this county and enrolled in our G.I. education classes thought so too." Zeno, whose determination was as fiery as his red hair, became their spokesman.

The Republicans rightfully considered these rumblings of dissatisfaction a threat to their control. They struck back by complaining to the government about the way the local veterans' classes were being run and were successful in closing down the classes.

Heated political meetings followed, along with an attempt to throw out the Board of Education members. At one meeting of the opposition, Ponder says, "A four-bushel catsack would not have held the pistols those fellows were carrying." But Ponder and his supporters were not easily frightened and their strength grew.

In 1950 Ponder was appointed precinct registrar. Unlike past registrars, he did not wait for people to come to him and register. He put the registration books in his car and drove to home after home getting voters registered. But the registration was still two Republicans for every Democrat.

That same year two Democrats won offices in the local election for the first time. One was elected sheriff by a thirty-two vote margin, while the other was elected to the state legislature. This was a great surprise to the Republicans. They not only contested the validity of the election, but the Republican "incumbent" sheriff refused to budge from his office. He holed up in the jail with a Tommy gun and pistols and would not let the new sheriff in.

While the legality of the election was being decided in court, some Democrats amused themselves nightly by riding past the sheriff's office and throwing a few firecrackers out the car window to shake the nerves of the former officeholder and make him think they were about to take the jail by force.

"We got a favorable verdict, though, in both superior court and the state supreme court, so our new sheriff finally took over his office," says Ponder lighting a cigarette and looking out the window of his den over the mountains. He is proud of the beautiful view from his home in all four directions.

About this time the new Democratic legislator introduced a bill in the state legislature requesting the establishment of a Tax Equalization Board to re-evaluate property. Democrats suspected Republican tax assessors of overvaluing property belonging to Democrats. The bill passed, and two Democrats and one Republican, with Ponder named as an assistant, began to re-evaluate property.

Being on friendly terms with the tax assessors can be very important in a small town. The value the tax assessor places on a man's property determines the amount of taxes he must pay. However, if a property owner feels he has been treated unjustly, he can appeal to the state.

In 1954 Zeno Ponder was appointed to his first position of real political power—chairman of the Board of Elections. He held this post for two years and during this time fired all the former registrars, replacing not only the registrars but also the judges (election judges may challenge a voter's right to vote, watch the balloting, and count the votes).

"Of course, I couldn't take the recommendations of the Republican party regulars in appointing new registrars and judges," explains Ponder.

Although in some counties the members of the County Board of Education run for election, in Madison County these are appointive offices which must be approved by the state legislature after a legislator from the county submits a list of names. Since a Democratic legislator was in office it is not surprising that Ponder was appointed chairman of the County Board of Education next. He had not only worked for the party but had long been interested in education.

Several of his supporters were also named to the board for in Ponder's words, "We tried to weed out those who had not been for progress and change and turn the school committees over to younger hands selecting people who wanted change."

WELCOME
• MENLO •
METHODIST
CHURCH
PASTOR

LEWIS POPE-PASTOR

MENLO
BAPTIST CHURCH
WELCOME

FRED W. BUCHANAN
PASTOR

SPEED
LIMIT
30

The Board of Education has the authority to hire and fire principals and teachers if it so desires.

The positions of chairman of the county election board and chairman of the county school board are two of the most powerful offices in any county. The first office, if not used with complete integrity, can be abused to influence election results. There is a small salary for the registrars and this extra money is always welcome as well as the chance to exercise a degree of power.

The county school board controls the jobs of teachers and principals all over the county.

Thus, Zeno Ponder is a man of considerable influence for a Democrat in a traditionally Republican county. Not until he ran for the state legislature did he hit a snag. He was charged with switching ballot boxes—four county precincts were in contention—and in one precinct, registrars were held at pistol point until members of the Board of Elections could arrive and confiscate the ballot boxes to check the number of ballots against the registrar's books.

Ponder's blue eyes look puzzled and hurt when he talks about the charge, which he denies vehemently. After much controversy his opponent was declared the winner.

But this has not stopped Ponder's civic and political work. He is presently secretary of the Democratic Executive Committee and president of the Madison County Development Board.

"I want to see our county have good roads and good schools," says Ponder, who has played an important part in the organization of a committee that is working toward consolidation of the five county high schools. And he continues to work for what he calls a "progressive political climate with healthy competition between both parties."

As they rounded the curve they came upon a hillside full of shacks with a pall of smoke hanging over it. A mine tipple stretched upward like a black skeleton against the sky.

James Callihan and his wife parked their old Ford, which had been overheating for the last twenty miles, and got out to look at the Kentucky coal camp. A cinder road wound like a twisting black snake up the hill toward the houses.

"We never should have left home," said his wife, Jessie. The baby she carried in the crook of her arm began to whimper and fuss.

Callihan was a tall, spare mountain man with tanned cheeks, bright blue eyes, and a thatch of sandy hair. He bent down wordlessly to pick a blade of grass to chew, saw the black coating and dropped it. Staring over at the side of the mountain, he took in the row upon row of grimy little boxes each exactly like the next. Below them was a railroad track and not far away he noticed a stream. For a moment he felt encouraged until he reached the bank and gazed down into the water flowing past, black and turgid. Sooty smoke from the burning slag pile hovered over the whole scene and all he could think of was the green cove they had left, the clear, sparkling streams, and the expanse of blue sky. They had owned a cow, but no cow could graze on grass like this. He was tired, hungry, infinitely discouraged and all around him instead of balsam forest or honeysuckle he could smell nothing but coal.

But the Big Ben Mine came to mean money, more cash money than they had ever had, at least for a while. After little Jamie had just begun to walk, Sarah was born. Then in regular succession came Johnny, Lem, Liza Jane, Billy, Rosie, and Jacob. Soon they were used to nobody owning his own house or store or land. Jessie bought everything from baloney to baby's clothes at the company store. The mining company also owned the church and everything else but the small schoolhouse, which was owned by the county. There was no library and no hospital.

There were still some black men working here at the Big Ben Mine, lured to the coal camp by rumors of high wages. But many

had become disillusioned by the miserable housing and harsh monotony of the coal camp and had left for the cities to find a better way of life.

Each day, with bread, ham, and apples in the dinner pail slung over his arm, Jim Callihan started out for the mine with the rest of the early morning shift. He would hear the rise and fall of the long, piercing shriek of the company siren summoning the men. He trudged along the cinder road, his heavy boots tipped with steel making a scrunching noise. On his head he wore a black metal hat.

Stopping at the "lamp house" he would pick up a four-pound electric battery, strap it around his waist, and plug in the long electric wire that hung from the lamp bulb in front of his hat. He never forgot one thing—to fasten to his belt the "self-rescuer." This was a sort of gas mask that would fit over his nose and give him enough oxygen to last forty-five minutes if an explosion filled the mine with gas—perhaps long enough to allow him to get to the entrance before being overcome by gas or flames. Callihan sometimes looked longingly at the green mountains in the distance but he was not sure what he would do if he returned. So, invariably he would turn his eyes back to the tall gray hills of slag, which looked more like the landscape of some long dead planet. This slag was a mixture of coal and slate that could not be used.

Callihan would crouch down in the mine-train so his hard hat would not hit the top of the roof of the tunnel. Then the train would enter the gaping black mouth of the mine, jolting and swaying from side to side. He could feel the flat, open car pick up speed as he travelled down through the jet black tunnel, rushing deeper and deeper into the earth. Then he would get out to walk or crawl through the tunnels, sometimes in ankle-deep water until, after threading one inky passageway of the maze after another, he found his room. The ceiling was often no more than three feet high and its walls were carved out of coal, slate, and stone.

The air was damp and in the blackness nothing could be seen

A typical present-day miner of West Virginia

beyond the range of the circle of light from the lamp on his hat. Except for the muted, distant *pick, pick, pick* from other rooms, it was quiet and cool. His shoulders, so sore at first, were becoming used to stooping under the low ceiling propped up by wooden posts. He was shown how to operate an eerie-looking electric machine that would cut into the coal, its teeth filling the air with powdery, black "bug dust" until Callihan would wet his handkerchief with water and tie it over his mouth.

He learned to "shoot": to drill a hole and thrust a stick of explosive just deep enough into the coal to blow large lumps onto the floor of his room so that he could load them. But unlike some men who loved the danger of it—one explosion could so easily trigger another if there were gas and dust in the air—Callihan was a thoughtful, gentle fellow who never sought out danger for its own sake.

Occasionally, his thoughts would dwell on stories his good friend, Tom Maleski, had told him about cave-ins, explosions, and the much dreaded "afterdamp." An explosion may be caused by methane gas, which is given off by the coal as it is being mined. These gas explosions may kindle coal-dust explosions, which are much more violent and widespread and have caused the loss of many lives.

The afterdamp is a mixture of deadly gases that occurs in the air following an explosion. Afterdamp has little oxygen in it and is high in carbon monoxide. It is a common cause of death after mine explosions.

"You don't never know how it's goin' to hit you. All you know is it'll kill you," Maleski would say shaking his shaggy gray head. "I've heard of 'em findin' guys just like they was when it hit 'em, ready to swing a pick or reachin' into their dinner pail. You'd think they was alive 'til you looked closer at 'em. Then you'd see they'd been dead for days. What a creepy feelin'." Tom Maleski's eyes would darken with a look as near to fear as the big man ever showed.

"A fellow can suffer and try to claw his way out, he may

just go to sleep forever, or he might be lucky enough to keep alive 'til the rescuers get to him. Oncet I went back in to help look. We got to the spot and found a whole bunch a guys lyin' all over the place. All of a sudden this fellow right next to my foot turns his head and looks up at me. I guess I hollered out. I couldn't help it. He was the only one still alive out of two hundred men."

One day Jim Callihan came back to work after a Thanksgiving vacation to find a sign on the mine entrance. The sign read "Mine Closed." No one had ever imagined this could happen and most of the men had spent all their money while on vacation.

Jim had a little money left and Tom Maleski knew of a small mine not far away. The two men were able to get work there but they soon learned that at this mine their membership in the United Mine Workers Union was no help. The mine had a wage contract with the union but ignored it, and the big union looked the other way. The coal company paid as little as it possibly could, usually from four to eight dollars a day.

Safety regulations were often disregarded and one day Jim almost lost his life. He was working on the "face" (where the coal was being dug), glancing up as usual at the wooden supports. Tom reminded him when it was time to eat. Jim had just started toward his dinner pail when he heard the noise of splitting timber and, looking over toward the face, he saw the roof cave in and dirt, rocks, and timber pour down covering his friend.

Callihan shouted for help and several other miners ran toward the cave-in. With pick and shovel the men dug desperately but when they finally reached Maleski it was too late. One of the timbers had shattered his head. From then on it wasn't that Jim Callihan was scared, it was just that he had lost heart. Wages grew lower and lower and at home there never seemed to be enough to eat or enough clothes and shoes to go around for himself, his wife, and eight children.

One Friday in the spring of 1959, Jim handed his pay envelope

over to Jessie and when she opened it and saw that he had only received twenty dollars for his week's work, she burst into tears and dropped the money on the floor.

This was the spring that John L. Lewis, longtime president and hero of the United Mine Workers, decided after ten years of silence to force the operators of the small pits to live up to their contracts with the miners.

"It's too late, Jessie. I just don't believe he's really for us anymore," said Callihan to his wife. She listened silently. The next day Jim went back to work at the mine. In a few days there was a line of pickets. Some of the men quit and joined them. The mine cut down to two or three days a week. Now, Jim was lucky to bring home twelve dollars. He had no savings nor did he own anything but his old car, and some money was better than none when you have a family to feed. "Scab!" the pickets shouted at him as he walked past their line to go to work. The pickets began to tangle with the coal police who were hired to break the strike. The state police came in and used tear gas. In county after county men were killed and mine tipples where coal is sorted were burned. The National Guard was called in to restore order and finally the strike failed because the men had lost faith in the union.

A few months later when Jim Callihan returned home one evening after work, he looked at the mountain across from his "four rooms and a path [outhouse]" to see a long scar across its face, two bulldozers, and a power shovel. The strip miners had begun their work. All day long Jessie could hear the boom of the explosives, and clouds of dust rose in the air as rocks and dirt were hurled down the mountainside. Trees, too, were pushed down the slope and a "highwall" of dirt rose forty feet in the air. Soon the dirt had washed down the mountainside and the stream at the bottom became a dammed-up pond where mosquitoes bred. Once-rich topsoil turned to sterile subsoil filled with fragments of stone and slate.

After the strip miners had left, the auger miners arrived with their gigantic drills, some of them as much as six feet wide.

They spewed out coal far faster than men in underground mines could mine it, fifteen tons in less than a minute. The operation was cheap and fabulously profitable, requiring only a few men. But fields became wastelands of soil and rock which had been washed down the mountainsides, and the mountains themselves were decapitated and shattered. After the strip and auger miners did their work, the land was reduced to a shambles.

It was not long before the Callihans, like other families who had stayed on in the area, decided to move. Stones fell on houses and there were avalanches of dirt. The land became worthless. Few companies made much of an effort to obey laws requiring them to replant the ravaged land. Actual restoration is prohibitively expensive, if not impossible.

Jessie thought Jim might find work as a bulldozer operator but he refused.

"When I come here those mountains was still covered with fine timber. Green in the summer and come fall they looked like nature was plumb shoutin' with color. You think I'm agoin' out there and slash 'em and cut their heads off. No!"

So, the Callihans moved with the others. Some went to cities, a few got jobs in bigger mines where here or there they found an opening, and others went on to another "dog hole" as they called the little mines.

Although there are still some big underground mining operations in Appalachia, the cheapness with which the stripper and auger miners can produce coal is gradually squeezing them out and more men are out of work. At the same time thousands of acres of land are being wrecked.

The book *Night Comes to the Cumberlands* by Harry Caudill gives a graphic description of how laws made for the purpose of restoring the land are circumvented. Says Caudill, "Little effort is made to reclaim or stabilize the land, and indeed reclamation is rarely possible once the surface has been so violently disturbed.

"Under the law, strippers are required to replant their wrecked and ravaged acres. The State Department of Conservation [Ken-

tucky] recommends short-leaf or loblolly pines for the spoil-banks. Conservationists insist that a full year must pass before the young trees are planted. This delay permits the freshly piled soil to settle enough so the trees can take root. The seedlings are approximately five inches long when planted, supposedly at intervals of six feet. Some ten years must elapse before trees growing in such impoverished earth will reach the height of a man's head. In the meantime the rains have clawed the earth about their roots into deep gullies and there is little left for their foliage to protect. Few operators seriously attempt to comply with the reclamation regulations; most are permitted to virtually ignore them."

As a result of the prodding of the United Mine Workers Union, legislation has been passed in many states to produce safer working conditions in the underground mines. Safety regulations have also been passed by the Bureau of Mines of the U. S. Department of Interior. It is one thing to pass safety laws, however, and another to be able to check every mine frequently enough to see that the coal companies are complying with the regulations. Another factor may be the reluctance of a miner to report bad conditions when his own foreman is conducting an inspector through the mine.

Coal companies do understand more now about the causes of mine accidents than was known in the past. Material is constantly being published by the Bureau of Mines to teach mine officials how to test for gas, how best to keep a steady flow of fresh air through the mine passages, decrease the possibility of roof cave-ins and lower the number of coal-dust explosions by blowing rock dust from a machine to coat the mine walls with powdered limestone.

But no matter how hard a company may try to eliminate hazards there will always be dangers in underground coal mining, and as a British team which visited our coal mines reports, "the purpose is to produce coal cheaply." Safety measures are expensive and so is restoring land damaged by strip

Strip-mining leaves ugly gashes in the Appalachian landscape

mining. This means less profit for the people who own the coal companies.

At least, the company store has become a thing of the past, the houses have been sold to the miners who live in them, and some companies even provide recreation facilities. But so many millions of dollars of profit have been taken out of the areas where the coal has been mined and the coal companies have put so little of the enormous wealth from this great natural resource back into these areas that the effect on both the people and the land has been devastating.

The American public enjoys the benefits of coal in the form of cheap electricity, plastics, dyes, nylon, synthetic rubber, drugs, and other products, but few of us realize the price we have paid in human lives lost in underground mining, entire communities displaced, and land rendered valueless by strip mining. People will not pay taxes on land which has been reduced to what Caudill terms "a colossal rubbish heap." Schools and other public facilities must go without desperately needed tax revenue and more prosperous areas of a state must help foot the bill.

Hopefully, the day will come soon when we are genuinely concerned about the people who live on this land and about the whole economy of these areas rather than simply the cheapest possible way of removing the coal from the ground.

"Then she come from around the bend and was making time down the gorge, puffing and a-smoking and a-steaming. She was a pretty sight and if I live to be a hundred I'll never forget her. She was sure shining, all green and red and silver with a big red and gold stack.

"Then there was the biggest thing of all. The engineer stuck his head out the window and waved and blew the whistle.

" 'Tweet,' it said, 'tweet, tweet, tweeeet'," recalls an old man who saw Tweetsie's first run in 1881.

And so the little train was nicknamed "Tweetsie" by the mountain people of Carolina and Tennessee who turned out all along the tracks to see her that summer of 1881. Few of them had ever seen a train before.

Fifty years later in the 1930s three small mountain boys, Harry, Grover, and Spencer Robbins, often rode Tweetsie from Boone, North Carolina, to the tiny village of Fosco to visit their grandmother.

"We would ride along and look at the farmers plowing and sometimes kids would run beside the train and they'd wave and we'd wave back. We got to know the conductor, and the engineer let us ride in the cab, even let us toot the whistle. It was a real adventure," says Harry Robbins.

But one night in 1940 the flood-swelled waters of the Watauga River rushed fiercely over her banks and by morning had torn out much of Tweetsie's track. A few years later, passenger service on the rest of the track stopped and to the sorrow of the children along its path, the train ran no more.

"In Carolina how it did rain, it took from us our little train," mourned a little girl named Annette Vance in her poem which was read at the Interstate Commerce Commission hearing. But the track was never repaired nor was passenger service continued.

"We didn't know what had happened to Tweetsie until we heard Gene Autry had bought it to use in movies in California," says Harry Robbins. By then he and his brothers had grown up and were in the lumber business.

"We began to think about that train and how we used to ride it when we were kids. It was like a member of the family.

"We didn't know exactly what we would do with the train but we sat down and wrote Autry a letter telling him how people up here felt about Tweetsie and asking him if we could buy it and bring it home. He wrote back saying he didn't want to take it away if people in the mountains wanted it."

The Robbins brothers brought Tweetsie home over the mountains. They repaired her ancient boiler, refurbished the shabby, dirty interiors of the old coaches, and painted the train a sparkling green. *Tweetsie Railroad* was lettered in gold on each coach and the engine sported shiny brass trim.

It was late summer of 1957 when the historic little train, which long years ago had been the first to cross the Blue Ridge Mountains, began her run on the track Grover Robbins had built. Leaving Tweetsie Station, which is a replica of one of the old depots on her original route, Tweetsie crossed a 225-foot trestle and chugged around Roundhouse Mountain. Oldtimers and children by the score came to ride her and hear the shrill, sweet tweet of her whistle fill the air. From that day on Tweetsie's popularity grew until she became one of the region's top tourist attractions.

On business for the lumber company the brothers travel widely outside Appalachia, stopping here and there, often in Florida and California, getting ideas. All three are soft-spoken and seemingly easy going but beneath the surface there is great drive and imagination. Each man is an individual with his own contribution to make to their enterprises.

Grover is an informal fellow with a like-me-as-I-am-or-leave-me sort of attitude. He is not a conformist. He doesn't own a suit and he won't wear hats. Dressed in a sweater and slacks he often looks as if he had just come in from the golf course. And after the success of Tweetsie, Grover and Harry did begin to enjoy playing more golf. One day they were playing a course near Boone and there were so many people ahead of them that they had to stop and wait at every hole. After the third one

Grover said, "To heck with this, we're going to build our own course." That afternoon the two brothers went out and bought the land.

"Then we didn't play so much. We had to promote it to pay for it," says Harry Robbins a bit ruefully.

Along with the building of the golf course came Hound Ears Club (named after a rock formation nearby) which the brothers decided should be built like a Swiss chalet. The clubhouse was so beautiful but so unlike other buildings in the area that local people smiled when they spoke of it and speculated about whether it would prove to be the Robbins brothers' folly.

The first day the club opened, Grover happened to be standing in the impressive lobby dressed in a sweater and slacks and wearing sneakers when a man drove up in a big Cadillac. He charged in booming out, "Where is somebody to carry my bags?" Grover strolled casually out to the car and brought in the bags. The man tipped him a dollar never realizing that he was tipping the owner of the club! The incident amused Grover immensely.

As soon as Hound Ears began to prosper, one of the first things Grover did was to buy an airplane. He had loved planes ever since he was in college and bought an old plane for seventy-five dollars, which he fixed up and flew. His new plane was a beautiful heliocourier, designed for short take-offs and landings. One Sunday afternoon he was about to take off when he noticed three mountain boys from nine to twelve watching from the edge of the road near the airstrip. He invited them to come along. At first, the boys who had never been more than fourteen miles from home were reluctant, but Grover talked them into it and they flew to Atlanta with him. This was the beginning of the Aero Club for boys at the nearby high school who were interested in aviation.

Hound Ears grew quickly as club members bought lots and built beautiful summer homes on the mountains overlooking the golf course and clubhouse. Local skeptics were astonished by the success of Hound Ears.

The brothers might easily have stopped here, but they did not. For they were already planning their most ambitious project: Beech Mountain, with the highest ski runs in the East, golf courses, resort homes, shops, modern airport, and the fabulously expensive monorail, which Grover decided would be the best way for people to travel from one activity area to another. Concepts were also being developed to build houses in a cluster with their natural wooded setting preserved so that they would not mar the appearance of the mountain. A man who works closely with Grover Robbins says, "He doesn't do anything the way anyone else does."

The way Grover, Harry, and Spencer Robbins do things has resulted in recreation dollars from all over the United States coming in to this part of Appalachia. At the same time the recreation industry is providing a wide variety of job opportunities for the people of an area which had been steadily losing population.

There is much natural wealth in the southern Appalachians. The rivers are a source of hydroelectric power when dammed; there is still commercial timber despite the reckless greed with which it was cut and carried off in the early days; and there are deposits of minerals. But the typical mine or logging operation is a relatively small enterprise compared to manufacturing standards.

Deposits of semiprecious stones and minerals like feldspar, mica, and talc are mined in North Carolina but they have not contributed much to the economy. Coal mining now provides only a small percentage of the income of Appalachia, and that mainly from four states—West Virginia, Kentucky, Virginia, and Tennessee.

Here and there are small industries which have sprung up through local efforts such as the promising Mato Company in Madison County. Norris Gentry, a heavy-set young man with black hair, is a native of the region who has returned to run this tomato-packing and -marketing operation which is adding thousands of dollars to the income of local farmers. Only a year

Small industry is beginning to contribute to the economy of Appalachia

out of college, Gentry is right on top of the many problems which must be met in running Mato Company. He also understands Appalachia.

"It's not that all the people up here want to stay the way we are. A lot of us want to see things change. We have a great many proud but poor people. They are not illiterate. They are concerned and politically active. But we are caught in a situation unfavorable to the development of a middle-class economy." Norris Gentry, like many other Appalachian businessmen, knows that natural isolation and poor roads have discouraged two-way contact with the outside world and that the land is not suited to mechanized farming.

The beauty of the mountains and year-round sports facilities are beginning to attract tourists during every season, however, and there is food on the shelf in more and more homes due to the growing recreation industry.

Grover Robbins of Tweetsie, Hound Ears, Beech Mountain, the Land of Oz, and Land Harbors of America Campgrounds, to mention just a few of his current projects, has more than imagination. He has an outlook that springs from his native mountain background. His first interest is people, his second the land and the way it is developed. There is always the personal element, the respect for human individuality, the desire to use natural resources in a way that will preserve beauty, and a love of both people and the land that refuses to see either exploited. These qualities embody the best in the character of his mountain forefathers.

The greatest difference between Grover Robbins and other mountain people is that his two-way contact with the outside world has kept him from being resigned to Appalachia staying as it is. When someone asks this man, who could easily have retired if he wanted to, why he is starting a new project, Grover answers, "I just like to make things happen." Fortunately for his section of Appalachia, he is also a man who wants to make things better.

14. THE TREE AND THE ROCK

On the windy side of a mountain where there is often barren rock, there is something awesome about finding a tree growing out of a boulder. With no fertile soil to feed them, the roots extend like long fingers clutching the rough surface of the rock for support and reaching deep down into its cracks for life-giving nourishment.

Its branches may be twisted ruthlessly by howling gales but they continue to stretch bravely upward toward the giver of life to both plant and man, the sun.

As the tree has been shaped by its battle with nature, so the lives of many people in Appalachia have been stunted by harsh, unyielding circumstances.

In the vastness of the Blue Ridge Mountains, the Black Mountains, the Smokey Mountains, and the Cumberland Mountains was the most rugged land the settlers of America ever encountered. A primeval forest cut off even the sunlight from the forest floor. Into this twilight land, where a man could not tell high noon from dusk and in many places could not see the sky for the forest above him, came the forefathers of the mountaineers.

After three hundred years in their beautiful hills, the wind of isolation still blows cruelly upon the mountain people. Separated from their neighbors by one range of mountains after another, they early developed the independence needed to survive, but progress did not follow.

Behind them they had left organized education and religion, society as it existed, and the comforting and refining influences of civilization. They were their own providers of food, their own doctors; they taught their own children and they were their own law.

Because it was incredibly difficult to send a child over rugged country to a school, there was little interest in education. Efforts were concentrated on day-to-day survival rather than preparation for the future. Tasks around the home or the farm were considered more important. Education was a frill that many

parents thought did not fit a boy or girl for the mountain way of life.

The first families settled on low, fertile bottomland close to a trail and near a stream where they could draw water. They farmed the hillsides rather than live on the hillsides and farm the bottomland. Moving into the wilderness to escape the way of life of the eastern cities, these people were never really farmers. Families were large and as the young people married it was common for them to settle in the same cove or valley, simply moving up the mountainside to farm higher ground. Without knowledge of contour farming, they allowed much of the rich topsoil to wash away, and so it became increasingly difficult to raise enough crops for their own family, much less enough to take to market.

Here again, the mountains were an obstacle. Although the climate was good for many crops, there were no roads to take crops to market. Trading centers did not spring up quickly in Appalachia, and even with the coming of hard-surface roads, many families had to drive for a long time to reach the nearest town.

The mountains also acted as a barrier to good health, and disease came to be accepted. Doctors seldom reached the more remote areas, and generations of people grew up with no medical care but home herb-doctoring.

Often unable to read or write and with no idea of the value of their immense forests of virgin timber or the rich coal veins beneath their land, the mountain people were thoroughly fleeced by land and mining companies. A tree eight feet in diameter was sold for as little as fifty cents which, if a number of trees were sold, seemed a fortune to a mountaineer. In one case an entire valley which was worth $25,000 an acre was sold for $300. So land, timber, and mineral resources worth fabulous sums of money slipped through the fingers of these basically honest people, who were unused to the ways of grasping businessmen seeking to exploit them. It is no wonder they became suspicious of outsiders and even regarded them as "furiners."

In one mountain county there is a good paved road leading down the valley to the school. That is, all but a mile of it is paved. Stopping at a local store, a traveller learns that the owner of the land along the unpaved portion would not sell a few feet of his property so that the road could be widened enough to be paved. His father had told him, "Never sell any of your land." This is a reaction to past exploitation which still lingers in the minds of many mountain people.

Those who go into Appalachia to help these people solve their problems must be willing to take time to gain their confidence. Mountain families cling to their traditions and new ideas are sometimes resented, much to the surprise of church and government workers. Many of the problems are similar to those of the big city ghettoes, but resistance to new ideas, little enthusiasm for education, and the difficulty of getting the independent mountaineers to work together may mean slower progress for Appalachia than for the city slums.

Change is on the way, though, even if it seems to come slowly compared with the outside world. And television is the biggest single influence, particularly on the young people.

During an Apollo moon exploration, one mountain child came to school and excitedly related all the details to his teacher. He would probably never have known about it if he had not seen it on television. For many families a daily paper is a luxury, but television is regarded as almost a necessity. A secondhand television set can be bought for fifteen or twenty dollars, and probably two-thirds of the families in Appalachia own one.

Television sets are also being placed in most of the schools, and teachers are making use of educational channels in their classrooms to supplement textbooks.

"Television is showing the people of Appalachia what they don't have before they know how to get it," says one Appalachian politician.

Despite this widespread lack of material things, there is much to appreciate about the mountaineer's way of life. If he is on his way to a meeting, it is more important to him to stop and help someone who needs him, than to be on time to the meeting. He takes time to make friends and is intensely loyal to them. Nor does he have to be constantly working or active in order to be happy. He can sit on his porch swing and look at his mountains and be content. He will play with his children and enjoy it, even make toys for them without worrying about the clock.

But the fact remains that more than a million people in Appalachia have no work and little hope. One of the keys to solving Appalachia's multiple problems could be the efforts of hundreds of enthusiastic VISTA (Volunteers In Service To America) workers. They are a new breed of young people who do not see life as a career ladder with rungs of success to climb. They care about what happens to people and they care enough to want to do something to make things better.

In an area where men and women have long been accustomed to joblessness, the Volunteers have taught adults to read; started job-training programs; helped to begin small-business loan centers; given advice on Social Security benefits; explained how to apply for surplus food under the Food Stamp Plan; built roads, schools, and bridges; promoted sewage facilities; and even established a girl's vocational school.

They are tutoring children, teaching shop classes, counselling in homemaking, health, budgeting, and consumer education, as well as providing numerous other services according to the special needs of a community or area.

Another development which holds promise for the future is the Federal Development Planning Committee for Appalachia which will bring together the states and the federal government in a regionwide effort to provide better vocational education, highways, and local access roads, more health facilities, and the wiser use of natural resources such as land, timber, and water. The success of these recommendations made in the Appalachian Regional Development Act of 1965 will depend on how generously the states and federal government continue to appropriate necessary funds to do the job. Considerable time and money

have been spent in government studies only to find that Congress was unwilling to appropriate funds to carry out the proposals that would solve a problem.

A President's commission (originally appointed by President John F. Kennedy) gave double priority to highway construction in Appalachia, and better roads are certainly needed. But roads alone will not bridge the economic gap between Appalachia and the rest of the United States unless the government is willing to grapple with the problems of the people. Better education, expertly administered job-training programs, and a healthy population able to take full advantage of such programs is the real answer.

Not only in Appalachia but in many underdeveloped countries we have operated on the theory that building roads would solve all the problems, but our fine highways (a monument to our concern) go right past the doors of shacks that are still filled with suffering and ignorance. And so our task is far from finished. Individuals are one of the most important resources of any region and it is our obligation to discover how we can best help them help themselves. This is the hardest part of all for it is far easier to build roads than to educate and train people; but only if we accept this larger task, will we be on the way to making Appalachia the "land of promise" that the President's commission has called it.

BIBLIOGRAPHY

BLYTHE, LEGETTE. *Mountain Doctor.* New York: Morrow, 1964.

BRITISH COAL MINING PRODUCTIVITY TEAM. *British Coal Mining Productivity Team* (which visited the United States in 1951). 21 Tothill Street, London S W 1; 2 Park Avenue, New York 16: Anglo-American Council on Productivity, 1951.

CAUDILL, HARRY M. *Night Comes to the Cumberlands.* Boston, Toronto: Little, Brown, and Company, 1962.

CAUDILL, REBECCA. *My Appalachia.* New York: Holt, Rinehart, and Winston, 1966.

COTHRAN, MARION B. *Buried Treasure.* New York: Coward-McCann, Inc. 1945.

DYKEMAN, WILMA. *The French Broad.* Knoxville: University of Tennessee Press, 1965.

FORD, THOMAS R. *The Southern Appalachian Region.* Lexington: University of Kentucky Press, 1962.

FROME, MICHAEL. *Strangers in High Places.* New York: Doubleday, 1966.

GILFILLAN, LAUREN. *I Went to Pit College.* New York: Literary Guild, 1934.

KEYES, REV. CHARLES A. *Parson of the Hills.* New York: Vantage Press, 1956.

PARRIS, JOHN. *Mountain Bred.* Asheville, N.C.: Citizen-Times Publishing Company, 1967.

PARRIS, JOHN. *Roaming the Mountains.* Asheville, N.C.: Citizen-Times Publishing Company, 1955.

RAINE, JAMES WATT. *The Land of the Saddle-Bags.* New York: Published jointly by Council of Women for Home Missions and Missionary Education Movement of the United States and Canada, 1924.

SCHEER, JULIAN and ELIZABETH MCD. BLACK. *Tweetsie.* Charlotte, N.C.: Heritage House, 1958.

SHARPE, BILL. *A New Geography of North Carolina.* Raleigh N.C.: Sharpe Publishing Co. 1961.

WELLER, JACK E. *Yesterday's People.* Lexington: University of Kentucky Press, 1966.

DATE DUE

FE 14 77			
MR 23 '84			
AG 27 '84			